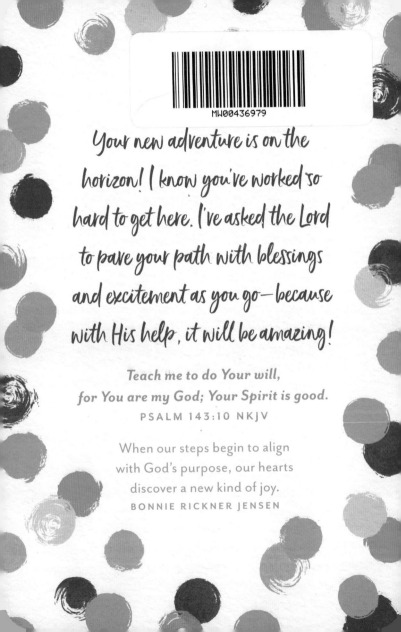

Your new adventure is on the horizon! I know you've worked so hard to get here. I've asked the Lord to pave your path with blessings and excitement as you go—because with His help, it will be amazing!

Teach me to do Your will,
for You are my God; Your Spirit is good.
PSALM 143:10 NKJV

When our steps begin to align
with God's purpose, our hearts
discover a new kind of joy.
BONNIE RICKNER JENSEN

It's so encouraging to see you live with joy and faith. Because you trust God more than the world, you just shine! I'm asking God to bless you with every answer to prayer and every blessing you could hope for.

And whatever you do, do it heartily, as to the Lord.
COLOSSIANS 3:23 NKJV

You are the only Bible some unbelievers will ever read.
JOHN MACARTHUR

Today is the happy result of so much hoping, working, dreaming, and believing. It's wonderful to see God's faithfulness through it all. I'm praising Him and celebrating you today!

This is a special day for the LORD, and He will make you happy and strong.
NEHEMIAH 8:10 CEV

There is no one who is insignificant in the purpose of God.
ALISTAIR BEGG

Making the right
choice can be hard when
other people are pushing for the
wrong one. But you have made the
hard decision to walk in integrity
and trust. I thank the Lord for His
grace in your life, and I've asked
Him to bless your good decisions!

*He fulfills the desires of those who
reverence and trust Him.*
PSALM 145:19 TLB

Be faithful in small things
because it is in them that your strength lies.
MOTHER TERESA

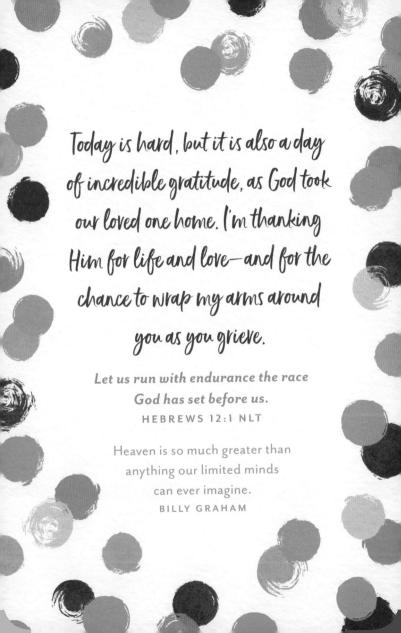

Today is hard, but it is also a day of incredible gratitude, as God took our loved one home. I'm thanking Him for life and love—and for the chance to wrap my arms around you as you grieve.

Let us run with endurance the race God has set before us.
HEBREWS 12:1 NLT

Heaven is so much greater than anything our limited minds can ever imagine.
BILLY GRAHAM

Wow, you made it through a very tough time! And now, as you are adjusting to the new, I'm asking Him to surround you with His love and protection.

We will shout for joy when you succeed, and we will raise a flag in the name of our God.
PSALM 20:5 NCV

You would never have known God's strength had His strength not been needed to carry you through.
CHARLES SPURGEON

We've been praying and trusting
God for big things, haven't we?
I know He hears and is answering.
I'll continue to trust, alongside you,
that He is hard at work!

*LORD, every morning You hear my voice.
Every morning, I tell You what I need,
and I wait for Your answer.*
PSALM 5:3 NCV

Give your hands to Him for His work,
your feet to walk His path, and your ears
to hear Him speak.
PRISCILLA SHIRER

I'm celebrating YOU
today, my friend!
You bring so much joy to
the world and the people you meet.
I've asked our Father
to double your blessings today,
in Jesus' name.

You shine as lights in the world,
holding fast the word of life.
PHILIPPIANS 2:15–16 NKJV

If more of us valued food and cheer
and song above hoarded gold,
it would be a merrier world.
J.R.R. TOLKIEN

I'm asking God to give you
the supreme satisfaction of
knowing you're making a
difference for Him.

I will bless you...
and you shall be a blessing.
GENESIS 12:2 NKJV

There are some needs only you can see.
There are some hands only you can hold.
There are some people only you can reach.
TIMOTHY KELLER

So much prayer has gone into this. And seeing our Father answer those prayers is an incredible gift. I'm thanking Him for listening to our hearts and for guiding us along the way.

Praying that all is well with you.
III JOHN 1:2 TLB

What wings are to a bird and sails to a ship, so is prayer to the soul.
CORRIE TEN BOOM

God is such a good Leader!
He's brought you to this very day
and moment, and it's amazing
to see how you're rocking it!
I'm thanking Him for His guidance
all the way through.
I'm celebrating Him for YOU!

Lead me in Your truth and teach me,
for You are the God of my salvation;
on You I wait all the day.
PSALM 25:5 NKJV

Relying on God has to start all over every day,
as if nothing has yet been done.
C. S. LEWIS

The Lord outdid Himself
when He made you,
and the world is so much better
because you're in it!
I'm praying that today
is a reminder to you of
how loved, special,
and on purpose you are.

The LORD your God chose you
to be His own. You belong to the LORD.
DEUTERONOMY 14:2 CEV

Be who God meant you to be and
you will set the world on fire.
CATHERINE OF SIENA

We know that everything God
ever promised has or will happen.
He's completely trustworthy. I've
asked God to bless you with a peace
that goes beyond any human
understanding.

Search the book of the Lord
and see all that He will do;
not one detail will He miss.
ISAIAH 34:16 TLB

Be. Be still. Be still and know.
Be still and know that I am.
Be still and know that I am God.
ROY LESSIN

I thank God for being so present in your life—I can't wait to see how it will all unfold, but I'm already celebrating the happy ending.

The LORD gives His people strength. The LORD blesses them with peace.
PSALM 29:11 NLT

If my life is once surrendered, all is well. Let me not grab it back, as though it were in peril in His hand but would be safer in mine!
ELISABETH ELLIOT

Wow! It's been amazing to watch
God's plan for you unfold.
I've told Him how happy I am
that He's showing you how much
He truly cares.

Every good action and
every perfect gift is from God.
These good gifts come down from
the Creator of the sun, moon, and stars.
JAMES 1:17 NCV

God's work done in God's way
will never lack God's supply.
HUDSON TAYLOR

You needed God to show
up and He did!
You needed a miracle, and He
knew it. I'm praising God for
loving you so deeply and meeting
your need so completely.
I'm celebrating
His faithfulness today.

The LORD shows His true love every day.
PSALM 42:8 NCV

If you believe in a God who controls the big
things, you have to believe in a God who
controls the little things. It is we, of course,
to whom things look "little" or "big."
ELISABETH ELLIOT

God has called you to great things!
It's exciting to watch. Today I asked
God to please stay close to you and
guide your every step.

If you seek Him, you will find Him.
1 CHRONICLES 28:9 NLT

This is our time on the history line of God.
This is it. What will we do with the
one deep exhale of God on this earth?
For we are but a vapor.
Direct us, Lord, and get us on our feet.
BETH MOORE

I'm thanking Him for
restoring your hope and I'm
praying He keeps you close
to His heart and surrounds
you with His amazing love.

You refresh my life.
You are true to Your name,
and You lead me along
the right paths.
PSALM 23:3 CEV

Don't worry about locating your
purpose. If you are seeking after God,
your purpose will locate you.
TONY EVANS

Change can be hard,
but God never changes!
I'm praying He will be
the steady hand in your
circumstances as He leads you
into amazing new things.

**Those who trust in the LORD
will renew their strength;
they will soar on wings like eagles.**
ISAIAH 40:31 CSB

Don't be afraid of change,
because it is leading you
to a new beginning.
JOYCE MEYER

*You have worked to
forgive, and it shows.
I'm asking the Lord to continue
to heal your heart and
your relationship.*

*You have lifted me up,
and have not let my foes
rejoice over me.*
PSALM 30:1 NKJV

Forgiveness unleashes joy.
It brings peace.
It washes the slate clean.
It sets all the highest values in motion.
GEORGE MACDONALD

Today I asked God to encourage you—because you bless and encourage so many others. You may not want to be recognized, but some of us can't help but notice what a wonderful gift of a human being you are.

Don't hide your light! Let it shine for all; let your good deeds glow for all to see, so that they will praise your heavenly Father.
MATTHEW 5:15–16 TLB

I am content to fill a little space if God be glorified.
SUSANNA WESLEY

I've asked God today to bless the work of your hands. I've asked Him to bring you success in whatever you set out to do.

God, our own God, shall bless us.
PSALM 67:6 NKJV

The Christian shoemaker does his duty not by putting little crosses on the shoes, but by making good shoes, because God is interested in good craftsmanship.
MARTIN LUTHER

I'm celebrating
your friendship today!
I am asking Him especially
to bless you, my friend,
who has made my life
so much sweeter.

*You are better off to have
a friend than to be all alone....
If you fall, your friend
can help you up.*
ECCLESIASTES 4:9–10 CEV

Kindness doesn't happen by accident.
MATT ANDERSON

God encouraged us to
hang in there, and now we
understand why, don't we?
What a great outcome!
It is a day to celebrate Him and
what He has done for us.
Thank You, Lord!

And the LORD, He is the one
who goes before you. He will be with you,
He will not leave you nor forsake you.
DEUTERONOMY 31:8 NKJV

Never give up, for that is just the place
and time that the tide will turn.
HARRIET BEECHER STOWE

Today I am asking God to lead us
to pray in ways that are in line
with His heart and what
He is doing in our lives and
the world around us.

*No good thing will He withhold
from those who walk along His paths.*
PSALM 84:11 TLB

God does not give us everything we want,
but He does fulfill His promises,
leading us along the best and
straightest paths to Himself.
DIETRICH BONHOEFFER

As you step out in faith, I'm asking Him to strengthen your courage and show you the way to go.

May you always be doing those good, kind things that show you are a child of God.
PHILIPPIANS 1:11 TLB

Your potential is the sum of all the possibilities God has for your life.
CHARLES STANLEY

Who would have
thought we'd have gotten
this far—and I know we
couldn't have without the Lord.
Today my prayer is
to be taken even further!

Blessed be the Lord,
who daily loads us with benefits.
PSALM 68:19 NKJV

Trust whatever He has for you.
It will be better than anything
you can plan for yourself.
FRANCIS CHAN

*May God continue
to help you learn and grow,
with humility and courage,
for years to come.*

*I know the thoughts that I think
toward you, says the LORD,
thoughts of peace and not of evil,
to give you a future and a hope.*

JEREMIAH 29:11 NKJV

You can't be who you are going to be
and who you used to be at the same time.

T.D. JAKES

I'm asking God to keep
you close to Him, leading
you clearly for the rest
of your life.

Your right hand supports me;
Your help has made me great.
You have made a wide path
for my feet to keep them
from slipping.
PSALM 18:35–36 NLT

Live near to God,
and so all things will appear
to you little in comparison
to eternal realities.
ROBERT MURRAY MCCHEYNE

Contentment is such
a gift from the Lord.
Today I asked the Holy Spirit
to help you find
His beauty in every day,
no matter what.

He who is of a proud heart stirs up strife,
but he who trusts in the LORD
will be prospered.
PROVERBS 28:25 NKJV

Contentment...has an internal quietness
of heart that gladly submits to God
in all circumstances.
JONI EARECKSON TADA

I'm celebrating your
sweet spirit and generous
heart today! I'm thanking God
for loving you so well that you
want to share what you have
received from Him.
You are a gift!

Let your light shine
for all the nations to see!
For the glory of the Lord
is streaming from you.
ISAIAH 60:1 TLB

A really great person is the person
who makes every person feel great.
GILBERT K. CHESTERTON

God is the God of brave things, and He helps us walk bravely through life. I've asked Him to be with you today as you strap on your armor and take courageous steps in faith-filled directions.

We put our hope in the LORD.
He is our help and our shield.
PSALM 33:20 NLT

We have to be braver than we think
we can be, because God is
constantly calling us to be
more than we are.
MADELEINE L'ENGLE

Let's celebrate God's perfect plans today! I'm thanking Him for using His all-seeing, all-knowing nature for our benefit. I know He's up to very good things, and that is cause for great joy!

We know that God is always at work for the good of everyone who loves Him. They are the ones God has chosen for His purpose.
ROMANS 8:28 CEV

We often don't realize that where God puts us is the very place we need to be to receive what He wants to give us.
PRISCILLA SHIRER

What a milestone
we are celebrating!
I'm thanking the Lord
for His faithfulness and
love through it all.

He is our God and
we are the people
He takes care of,
the sheep that He tends.
PSALM 95:7 NCV

God will not be behind-hand in love to us:
for our drop, we shall receive an ocean.
THOMAS WATSON

*God is so good to turn
our mustard-seed faith
into something amazing.
For that I am thanking Him today!*

*God is faithful,
by whom you were called
into the fellowship of His Son,
Jesus Christ our Lord.*
I CORINTHIANS 1:9 NKJV

If you can't fly, then run.
If you can't run, then walk.
If you can't walk, then crawl.
But whatever you do,
you have to keep moving forward.
MARTIN LUTHER KING JR.

My, oh my, what a dream-come-true this is—and it wouldn't have, couldn't have, happened without Him! I'm celebrating with joy and thanking Him from the bottom of my heart!

Love Him and serve Him with all your heart and soul.
DEUTERONOMY 10:12 NLT

God has a dream for you, your talents, your one life that never has been and never will be duplicated by anyone else.
HOLLEY GERTH

God has clearly helped you do a hard thing, and the victory is sweet! As you move forward today, I'm asking Him to help you keep that sense of wonder and joy.

The LORD directs the steps of the godly. He delights in every detail of their lives.
PSALM 37:23 NLT

Every time you look in the mirror, remember that God created you and that everything He creates is beautiful and good.
JOYCE MEYER

DaySpring

What a gift,
to follow a trustworthy God.
I know He's lifting you up.
I believe that together,
you and He are unstoppable!

The LORD is good....
Every day He can be trusted.
ZEPHANIAH 3:5 NCV

When we believe in the impossible,
it becomes possible,
and we can do all kinds
of extraordinary things.
MADELEINE L'ENGLE

DaySpring

Today I'm praising God
for answered promises.
He doesn't have to love us
the way He does—
but He does!

*All of God's promises
have been fulfilled in Christ
with a resounding "Yes!"*
II CORINTHIANS 1:20 NLT

Sometimes God lets you
hit rock bottom so that
you will discover that
He is the Rock at the bottom.
TONY EVANS

DaySpring

I know God sees the big picture, and He knows what we don't. He lets us know what we need to in order to thrive by His plans. It's comforting to know He is in control!

Your kingdom is an everlasting kingdom, and Your dominion endures throughout all generations.
PSALM 145:13 NKJV

Where you end up going and what you end up doing ultimately matters less than who you end up becoming.
MATT ANDERSON

I am celebrating God's love
for you today!
A big thanks to Him
for caring so deeply
about your personal needs
and desires. What an
incredible Father we have!

**In Him our hearts rejoice,
for we trust in His holy name.**
PSALM 33:21 NLT

The only person who dares wake up a king at
3:00 AM for a glass of water is a child.
We have that kind of access.
TIMOTHY KELLER

I'm praising God for
good friends like you!
Our lives are changed for the better
by the ones who live generously
and demonstrate His goodness—
and that describes your role
in my life, friend.

A friend loves at all times.
PROVERBS 17:17 CSB

Goodness consists not
in the outward things we do,
but in the inward thing we are.
EDWIN HUBBELL CHAPIN

What a generous God He is!
There's so much to celebrate—
so we're celebrating Him
in a big way today!

You were precious in My sight,
you have been honored.
ISAIAH 43:4 NKJV

Rejoicing is grounded in gratitude,
with a keen appreciation for yourself,
others, your abundance,
and the beauty around you.
SUSAN C. YOUNG

I'm thanking God
for the exciting ways
He's working
in your life!

**May the LORD give you
all that you ask for.**
PSALM 20:5 NCV

God doesn't expect
the impossible from us.
He wants us to expect
the impossible from Him!
DWIGHT L. MOODY

The Lord's blessings are
so evident in your life,
and I'm celebrating all He's given!
I've asked Him today to continue
answering your prayers and
accomplishing all you hope for.

**God's blessings
are given to us by faith,
as a free gift.**
ROMANS 4:16 TLB

We serve a God
who is waiting to hear from you,
and He can't wait to respond.
PRISCILLA SHIRER

It's a day to rejoice in
kindness and love, grace
and confidence in the Lord.
People like you are some of
His best inventions!

*Happy are those who are strong
in the Lord, who want above all else
to follow Your steps.*
PSALM 84:5 TLB

Encourage everyone you meet
with a smile or compliment.
Make them feel better
when you leave their presence
and they will always be glad
to see you coming.
JOYCE MEYER

God saw it too—the way you stepped up to the plate in a challenge. I saw His peace there, strengthening you. And I have thanked Him for His peace on your behalf!

Now may the God of hope fill you with all joy and peace in believing, that you may abound in hope by the power of the Holy Spirit.
ROMANS 15:13 NKJV

Peace doesn't mean that you will not have problems. Peace means that your problems will not have you.
TONY EVANS

Weakness is a hard thing to be happy about—except when we remember that He is our strength. Your willingness to be "weak" has strengthened your character and situation—and that's a reason to celebrate!

Because He bends down to listen, I will pray as long as I have breath!
PSALM 116:2 NLT

The weaker I am, the harder I must lean on God's grace; the harder I lean on Him, the stronger I discover Him to be, and the bolder my testimony to His grace.
JONI EARECKSON TADA

Oh, how your light shines BRIGHT!
God has given you
what you need to make such
a difference in the world.
I'm celebrating the way you are
bringing Him glory!

Our God, who is full of kindness through
Christ...will come and pick you up,
and set you firmly in place,
and make you stronger than ever.
I PETER 5:10 TLB

Let's turn our eyes away from the darkness
and turn them toward the Light and the Hope.
KATY FULTS

Seeing God's blessings
"at work" in your life,
in the form of amazing gifts
and talents, is a blessing in itself.
I'm asking Him to continue filling
you with His sweet love.

You bless the godly, O LORD;
You surround them with
Your shield of love.
PSALM 5:12 NLT

There is no one
who is insignificant
in the purpose of God.
ALISTAIR BEGG

You made a big decision, and the Lord was with you all the way! I'm asking Him to keep leading you through this time. May He keep showing you, time and again, that He is near and that He cares.

If you want to know what God wants you to do, ask Him, and He will gladly tell you.

JAMES 1:5 TLB

If the Lord be with us, we have no cause
for fear. His eye is upon us, His arm over us,
His ear open to our prayer—
His grace sufficient,
His promise unchangeable.

JOHN NEWTON

Oh boy, what joy! What a sweet end to an up-and-down journey. Or is this just the beginning? I can't wait to see what He's going to do next in your life.

A desire accomplished is sweet to the soul.
PROVERBS 13:19 NKJV

Obstacles are those frightful things you see when you take your eyes off the goal.
HANNAH MORE

I'm thanking God
for the gift of amazement,
and asking Him to keep us
guessing at what beauty and
surprises He'll send our way next.

The LORD's love never ends;
His mercies never stop.
They are new every morning.
LAMENTATIONS 3:22–23 NCV

Heart of mine—be amazed by grace,
be captivated by mercy,
be content in everlasting love.
ROY LESSIN

God's plans for you are
so good! I've thanked Him
for having His best in mind
for you—and for loving you
so personally and leading you
in His perfect way.

Those who listen
to instruction will prosper;
those who trust the LORD
will be joyful.
PROVERBS 16:20 NLT

Always, everywhere God is present,
and always He seeks to discover Himself
to each one.
A. W. TOZER

It may not be what you expected,
but I'm praying you'll discover
His full purposes, grace,
and peace on this journey.

**When troubles come your way,
consider it an opportunity for great joy.
For you know that when your faith is
tested, your endurance has
a chance to grow.**
JAMES 1:2–3 NLT

Rejoice in small things and
they will continue to grow.
SLAVEN VUJIC

Life is so full of goodness! It's a great day to celebrate life, friends, family, and love. So I'm praising God, the Giver of all the best gifts, for all the good things He's sent your way.

The LORD will protect you and keep you safe from all dangers. The LORD will protect you now and always wherever you go.
PSALM 121:7–8 CEV

Real value isn't in what you own, drive, wear, or live. The greater value is found in love and life, health and strength, friends and family.
T. D. JAKES

The Lord is the inventor
of good ideas—and you are
one of His best! I'm asking Him
to remind you today of
what a good idea you are.

The LORD has promised good things.
NUMBERS 10:29 NKJV

I would rather be what God chose
to make me than the most glorious creature
that I could think of; for to have been thought
about, born in God's thought, and then made
by God, is the dearest, grandest, and most
precious thing in all thinking.
GEORGE MACDONALD

Some of God's best work
is in the smallest details—
and He tends to fill our lives to
overflowing with those.
I'm asking God to open your eyes
to all of His many, personalized
blessings today.

Accept our praise, O Lord,
for all Your glorious power.
We will...celebrate Your mighty acts!
PSALM 21:13 TLB

Our Lord has written the promise of
resurrection, not in books alone,
but in every leaf in springtime.
MARTIN LUTHER

It's so fun to watch you
in your element.
I'm praying God helps you
thrive in your gifts and
truly enjoy every moment!

In His grace, God has given us different
gifts for doing certain things well.
ROMANS 12:6 NLT

Start by doing what's necessary;
then do what's possible;
and suddenly you are doing
the impossible.
FRANCIS OF ASSISI

God utterly outdid Himself
when He created you and
guided you to this point in
your life. And for that I am
thanking Him today!

You saw me before I was born
and scheduled each day of my life
before I began to breathe....
How precious it is, Lord,
to realize that You are thinking
about me constantly!
PSALM 139:16–17 TLB

Our ultimate purpose in life
is to glorify God.
BENJAMIN WATSON

DaySpring

What an amazing, wonderful day it is—and what an amazing, wonderful God we serve. Every ounce of praise to Him as we rejoice right along with you.

**You can get anything—
anything you ask for in prayer—
if you believe.**
MATTHEW 21:22 TLB

Any faith in Him, however small,
is better than any belief about Him,
however great.
GEORGE MACDONALD

Some decisions in life
are so important—and
you've just made one of the best!
As I celebrate your decision today,
I'm thanking God for leading you
to this very moment.

*Your word is a lamp to my feet
and a light to my path.*
PSALM 119:105 NKJV

Seek God, not happiness—this is the
fundamental rule of all meditation.
If you seek God alone, you will gain
happiness: that is its promise.
DIETRICH BONHOEFFER

What we thought could never happen—DID! And even as we're giving God ALL the credit, we're thanking Him for the amazing ways He's been at work in your life.

Overwhelming victory is ours through Christ.
ROMANS 8:37 NLT

There is nothing impossible with God. All the impossibility is with us when we measure God by the limitations of our unbelief.
SMITH WIGGLESWORTH

God is always faithful.
Today I've taken special time
to ask Him to remind you of
His faithfulness—in your
life and the lives of the ones
you love.

Let me experience Your faithful
love in the morning, for I trust in
You. Reveal to me the way I should
go because I appeal to You.
PSALM 143:8 CSB

Faith sees the invisible,
believes the unbelievable,
and receives the impossible.
CORRIE TEN BOOM

We're applauding big time,
and the accolades are huge!
When God created you,
He outdid Himself!

**Before I was born,
God chose me and called me
by His marvelous grace.**
GALATIANS 1:15 NLT

Remember who you are.
Don't compromise for anyone,
for any reason. You are a child
of the Almighty God.
Live that truth.
LYSA TERKEURST

When God does such
wonderful things for
someone we care so much about
(YOU), that's certainly a reason
to celebrate! We're praising God—
Hip, hip, hooray!—
for His amazing work
in your life.

With men it is impossible,
but not with God; for with God
all things are possible.
MARK 10:27 NKJV

I am always content with what happens;
for I know that what God chooses is better
than what I choose.
EPICURUS

I'm praising God today
for showing up and
shining bright
through YOU!

God is working in you,
giving you the desire and
the power to do what pleases Him.
PHILIPPIANS 2:13 NLT

Your job is not to produce the light,
it is simply to shine His light.
You just be you,
and He will do the rest.
APRIL RODGERS

The goal was big, but your faith was bigger—and God's blessings are bigger still! Congratulations on holding on, hanging in, and having an amazing story to tell. I'm asking God to reward your faith big time!

By Your own hand You satisfy the desires of all who live.
PSALM 145:16 CEV

The Christian who walks with the Lord and keeps constant communion with Him will see many reasons for rejoicing and thanksgiving all day long.
WARREN WIERSBE

The Lord gives us special occasions.
He gives us special people.
And sometimes, He gives us both!
This is definitely a day for
rejoicing and saying thank you
to Him, on your behalf!

*My God will use His wonderful riches
in Christ Jesus to give you
everything you need.*
PHILIPPIANS 4:19 NCV

All that we have, all that we can be,
is the working of God's amazing grace.
MELISSA REAGAN

We've been waiting,
praying, anticipating...
and now we're celebrating.
Only God could have orchestrated
this moment in time—
and I'm praising Him for
all that He has done.

Our God, we give You thanks.
I CHRONICLES 29:13 GNT

God will meet you
where you are in order
to take you where
He wants you to go.
TONY EVANS

I'm thanking God today
for people like you
who are put on this earth
to make major differences.

*The person who plants a lot
will have a big harvest.*
II CORINTHIANS 9:6 NCV

Authentic ministry is both
an expression of the cross of Christ—
laying down one's life out of love for another;
and the resurrection power of God—
rolling away stones to bring
true freedom.
MATT ANDERSON

There's no doubt that God made you for a glorious PURPOSE. Today I asked Him to continue to lead you in His wonderful PLAN!

I will be your God
throughout your lifetime....
I made you, and I will care for you.
ISAIAH 46:4 NLT

To be really great in little things,
to be truly noble and heroic
in the insipid details of everyday life,
is a virtue so rare as to be
worthy of canonization.
HARRIET BEECHER STOWE

Today is a great day
for celebrating the
adventure of life with God!
Keep letting Him lead,
and I'll be praying as you go!

See how very much
our Father loves us,
for He calls us His children,
and that is what we are!
I JOHN 3:1 NLT

Jesus promised His disciples three things—
that they would be completely fearless,
absurdly happy, and in constant trouble.
GILBERT K. CHESTERTON

I'm thanking God
for filling your life
with deep satisfaction
and great joy.

Enjoy the good life…
every day of your life.
PSALM 128:5 THE MESSAGE

Contentment is not an issue of lifestyle—
it's an issue of life Source.
A drink from His river of Life brings
a satisfaction this world
will never understand.
ROY LESSIN

There are good times.
There are great times.
And then there are
times like this! So much
celebrating going on here,
because of Your amazing
grace. Thank You, Lord!

**Your God...will rejoice
over you with gladness.**
ZEPHANIAH 3:17 NKJV

The chief purpose of life, for any of
us, is to increase according to our
capacity our knowledge of God by all
means we have, and to be moved by it
to praise and thanks.
J.R.R. TOLKIEN

DaySpring

I'm shouting
God's praise today!
You have so much
to celebrate!

Thus I will bless You
while I live;
I will lift up my hands
in Your name.
PSALM 63:4 NKJV

God loves each of us
as if there were only one of us.
AUGUSTINE

I've prayed the Lord
would bless your day with
many beautiful things.
And I've asked Him to help you
feel His loving presence
as He guides you throughout
the years to come.

Of His fullness
we have all received,
and grace for grace.
JOHN 1:16 NKJV

Joy is the most infallible sign
of the presence of God.
UNKNOWN

I'm asking God to give you
BLESSING everywhere you look...
HAPPINESS around each corner...
FELLOWSHIP of the deepest kind...
LOVE poured out on you.

God's love has been
poured out in our hearts.
ROMANS 5:5 CSB

He is faithful to guide us and to love us,
so I'm entrusting my life and
my worries to Him.
We've got this.
KATY FULTS

There's definitely more love in this world because God made wonderful you. I'm grateful to Him for using you so faithfully and blessing the world so beautifully!

Because of what Christ has done, we have become gifts to God that He delights in.
EPHESIANS 1:11 TLB

God's definition of what matters is pretty straightforward. He measures our lives by how we love.
FRANCIS CHAN

Today, I'm thanking God
for showing up in
the tiniest details of your life.
The smallest joy is
cause for rejoicing.

God's peace, which is so great
we cannot understand it,
will keep your hearts and minds
in Christ Jesus.
PHILIPPIANS 4:7 NCV

In winter, on the darkest nights,
one rejoices even to see
the tiniest sliver of a moon.
MARTY RUBIN

*I am confident of this,
that God is rejoicing over
your life…working out His purpose
in you and pouring out more
blessings than you could imagine!
I'm giving Him PRAISE
for His good work!*

*The LORD bless you and keep you;
the LORD make His face shine upon you,
and be gracious to you; the LORD
lift up His countenance upon you,
and give you peace.*
NUMBERS 6:24–26 NKJV

He who lays up treasures in heaven looks
forward to eternity; he's moving daily
toward his treasures.
RANDY ALCORN

It's such a blessing to see the Lord
at work in your life...
answering prayers, fulfilling
hopes, granting dreams. And I'm
praying that He will continue
leading you faithfully.

You refresh my life.
You are true to Your name,
and You lead me along the right paths.
PSALM 23:3 CEV

God never said that the journey
would be easy, but He did say that
the arrival would be worthwhile.
MAX LUCADO

My heart is overjoyed to see God bless you with your dream-come-true! I'm asking Him to keep the blessings coming!

I can do all things through Christ who strengthens me.
PHILIPPIANS 4:13 NKJV

Those blessings are sweetest that are won with prayers and won with thanks.
THOMAS GOODWIN

Celebrating your achievement
brings two things to mind—
what a wonderful God we serve,
and what an incredible person
you are.

**God, our God,
will richly bless us.**
PSALM 67:6 NLT

The more we enjoy of God,
the more we are ravished with delight.
THOMAS WATSON

Wow, the Lord's great love is so evident in your life! I'm thanking Him for His amazing love!

God is love.
If we keep on loving others,
we will stay one in our hearts with God,
and He will stay one with us.
1 JOHN 4:16 CEV

God and love are synonymous.
Love is not an attribute of God, it is God.
Whatever God is, love is.
OSWALD CHAMBERS

What a celebration!
What a fancy day!
We waited, prayed, and trusted—
and the Lord came through.
Hooray!

*But the Holy Spirit produces this kind
of fruit in our lives: love, joy, peace,
patience, kindness, goodness, faithfulness,
gentleness, and self-control.*
GALATIANS 5:22–23 NLT

Never think that God's delays are God's
denials. Hold on; hold fast; hold out.
Patience is genius.
GEORGES LOUIS BUFFON

It's been so hard to see where things were heading—but here we are! I'm praying this sweet ending is just the beginning of the wonderful places He is going to take you next.

Nothing in all creation is hidden from God's sight.
HEBREWS 4:13 NIV

Faith is not a sense, nor sight, nor reason, but taking God at His word.
ARTHUR BENONI EVANS

You've worked so hard and used your God-given gifts to accomplish so much. Today we celebrate the accomplishment—the person (YOU!)—and the God who made it possible!

Each of you has been blessed with one of God's many wonderful gifts to be used in the service of others. So use your gift well.

1 PETER 4:10 CEV

Our role is not to show off; it's just to show up.

HOLLEY GERTH

Kudos to a BIG God
for making BIG things
happen! I'm so excited
to see things unfold in your life.
Way to go, God!

Now all glory to God, who is able,
through His mighty power at work
within us, to accomplish infinitely more
than we might ask or think.
EPHESIANS 3:20 NLT

If God is your partner,
make your plans BIG!
D. L. MOODY

This joyful moment
has come from sadness—
and I'm praising God
for turning ashes into beauty!

*I will comfort them
and turn their sorrow
into happiness.*
JEREMIAH 31:13 CEV

He is no fool who gives
what he cannot keep,
to gain what he cannot lose.
JIM ELLIOT

A perfect parking spot, a pretty flower, a chocolate cookie, an extra hour. I'm praising God for the little things He gives to make every day a day for joy!

The heavens declare the glory of God; and the firmament shows His handiwork.
PSALM 19:1 NKJV

Find joy in the ordinary.
MAX LUCADO

Today I'm celebrating you,
a very special person
who reflects God's heart
so beautifully every single day.

Kind words are like honey—
sweet to the soul and
healthy for the body.
PROVERBS 16:24 NLT

Let your words
be the genuine picture
of your heart.
JOHN WESLEY

There He goes again!
Reminding us of His
faithfulness! He's taken what
we see, added it to what we trust,
and made the most beautiful
results. I'm praying
in thanks today!

Faith is the confidence that
what we hope for will actually happen;
it gives us assurance about things
we cannot see.
HEBREWS 11:1 NLT

Take a saint, and put him into any condition,
and he knows how to rejoice in the Lord.
WALTER CRADOCK

The Lord created kindness as a knife that can cut through any dismal darkness. I'm thanking God for the kindness you showed me today. It didn't go unnoticed.

Whatever is born of God overcomes the world. And this is the victory that has overcome the world— our faith.

I JOHN 5:4 NKJV

How beautiful a day can be when kindness touches it.

UNKNOWN

God has blessed your socks off! He's surprised you with favor! He's let His goodness shine through in ways you never imagined. I'm rejoicing in the ways He has made Himself known in your life!

We walk by faith, not by sight.
II CORINTHIANS 5:7 NKJV

Christ literally walked in our shoes.
TIM KELLER

There are few things that bring
greater satisfaction than to spread
our wings of adventure and
reach a brand-new height!
Thanking God for helping you
take off.

*In everything You do, You are kind and
faithful to everyone who keeps our
agreement with You.*
PSALM 25:10 CEV

[Believers] have joy and comfort—
that joy that angels cannot give and
devils cannot take.
CHRISTOPHER FOWLER

DaySpring

Something so nice couldn't have happened to anyone nicer! I've prayed for you today, thanking God for the blessings He's given and asking Him to keep them coming.

Good people will be remembered as a blessing.
PROVERBS 10:7 NCV

God has given us two hands, one to receive with and the other to give with.
BILLY GRAHAM